GW00802276

A Beautiful Endeavour

Pursuing a Conversation about Same-Sex Attraction and Following Jesus

Stephen Elmes

creative tension publications

Text copyright © Stephen Elmes 2019
The author asserts the moral right to be identified as the author of this work.

All rights reserved. No part of this publication may be reproduced, stored in a retrieval system, or transmitted in any form or by any means – electronic, mechanical, photocopy, recording, or any other – except for brief quotations in printed reviews, without the prior permission of the publisher:

creative tension publications
1 Nelson Cottages, Oakdene Road
Bookham
Surrey KT23 3HD
United Kingdom
Tel: +44(0)1372453243

ISBN 978-1-9160669-0-8

All Scripture references are taken from the Holy Bible, Today's New International Version (TNIV), Cambridge University Press, © International Bible Society, Cambridge 2005.

WATCH THE VIDEOS!

A live performance of *A Beautiful Endeavour* has been captured in seven short videos, which you can access via my Facebook page (go to videos):

www.facebook.com/revstephenelmes

OR

On my YouTube channel (search for Stephen Elmes on Youtube and select the video series 'A Beautiful Endeavour').

This short book is a good companion to the video series, giving prompts for reflection and discussion, along with some extra resources.

An ideal resource for individuals, church leadership teams and home groups.

COMMENDATIONS

"In October of 2019, the Eastern Baptist Association offered four conversation days for Baptist ministers and leaders, led by Steve. We had over 100 attend. The days flowed really well, enabling good and honest conversation between the participants without demanding that anyone hold to or change to a particular viewpoint. Steve's approach demonstrated that it is possible to hold differences of conviction well on this and other subjects. I heartily commend Steve and these Beautiful Endeavour days to you."

Rev. Nick Lear, Regional Minister, Eastern Baptist Association, UK.

Praise for Stephen's first book, 'Sexuality, Faith & the Art of Conversation – Part One:

"Stephen Elmes' careful, caring, and thoughtful approach to this charged topic is not only rooted in a readiness to listen to different views but also to accurately represent them. What emerges is a model of biblically faithful, pastorally involved engagement that points a way forward not only on this issue but on many others.'

Mark Greene, Executive Director of the London Institute for Contemporary Christianity (LICC).

CONTENTS

Introduction   1

Scene One   5

Scene Two   7

Scene Three   9

Scene Four   13

Scene Five   15

Scene Six   18

Scene Seven   19

Join the Conversation   21

Resources for Delving Deeper   29

Appendix 1: Five Christian Viewpoints   31

Appendix 2: Alternative Scripts for Scenes Two & Three   34

Appendix 3: Guidance from the Wider Baptist Family   41

Sexuality, Faith & the Art of Conversation (Samples)   45

-- Chapter Four (of Part 1)   47

-- Chapter Five (of Part 1)   57

Parts Two, Three & Four – Introduction   71

Notes   74

ACKNOWLEDGMENTS

To Sara, for giving me the time needed to develop this story.

To all who have shared their stories with me.

To Andy Gill for his excellent work on the cover design.

To the ace team at Liquona for capturing the story on video, with special thanks to Matt Day for his filming prowess, and Robyn Rackley for her skillful and artistic editing.

To Sonia Tuttiett for her lovely needlework designs.

Let the beauty of the Lord our God be upon us.
Establish Thou the work of our hands;
establish Thou the work of our hands, dear
Lord.

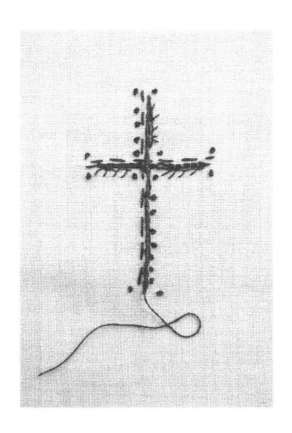

A Celtic Prayer [1]

INTRODUCTION

Recently I took a train towards London and got talking to a fellow passenger. Our conversation took in our families, our work, our thoughts about looking after the planet, and faith. When I asked Bryony what she thought about faith and church, she told me that she used to be involved but gave it up 'due to all the rules and because of the way the church treats people who are different – *especially those who are gay.*' These were almost her last words to me as the train pulled into my station, and I only had time to say that I hoped we might talk again…

As I walked from the station, I reflected on Bryony's view of the church. It was a sweeping judgement, of course, yet not without some basis in truth. Through the centuries and in our own time, the church has not always proclaimed or lived the gospel (good news) well in respect of those who experience same-sex attraction and may identify as gay. At times we have been condemning or insensitive or simply unwelcoming. Or else we have just avoided issues of sexuality and gender, leaving some among us to struggle secretly with feelings and desires that seem at odds with their faith. In some cases this has led to tragic consequences, as in the widely-reported case of Lizzie Lowe.[2]

For the last nine years, I have been involved in some practical research into how churches might respond well to those who are same-sex attracted and seeking to follow Christ.[3] This began with some theological and pastoral reflections within my own church community, which led to a dissertation, which became a book: *Sexuality, Faith & the Art of Conversation – Part One.*[4]

My work in this area has often involved helping churches get into honest and courageous conversations. There are significant pressures in the wider culture, as well as within the Christian community, that threaten to forbid or inhibit such discourse. On the one hand it can be deemed socially or politically offensive to be less than fully inclusive; on the other it can be seen as heretical or unfaithful to be asking questions of what the Bible teaches about same-sex attraction and behaviour.

So it has been something of a mission of mine – God given I trust – to help Christians make the space and summon the courage for a timely and vital conversation. I have been delighted often with the way people have engaged with the Scriptures and with each other. Some express deep relief at being able to talk about sexuality and faith in a safe context – to share concerns and questions. Always there is the realisation that Christ's followers hold a range of viewpoints and convictions about what it means for those who are same-sex attracted to follow Christ. Which, in turn, leads to a vital question for our churches: how do we hold our differences on this issue (and others) in a way that is Christ-like?

It is with this question in mind that I offer this resource to church leaders and communities, and others who are interested.[5] It comes in the form of a story – set out in seven scenes. It might best be described as a distillation of insight and wisdom gained from a good number of encounters with individuals and groups, including church leaders and communities, and those who identify as gay. I believe it may serve to represent some of the best endeavours of Christians to have this vital conversation in Christ-like fashion. I hope that it will inspire you to add your own voice, heart and best endeavours in Christ's name.

Let me give you just a few words about how to use this resource. I would like to encourage you first to read the story in one sitting – it will take no more than half an hour. Then read it scene-by-scene, pausing to reflect after each one, capturing your thoughts and reactions – perhaps in the spaces within this book, or using a journal or notepad. You might like to join with others to share these and get into conversation together. I have prepared this material with both individual and group participation in mind.

After the story, I have set out some prompts for reflection and discussion for each scene (*Join the Conversation*), as well as some recommended resources for delving deeper into the issues raised. At the end I have included some sample chapters of my book, *Sexuality, Faith & the Art of the Conversation – Part One*, and the introduction to *Parts Two, Three and Four* (the follow up volume).

Enough preambles.

If you are sitting comfortably – then I will begin…

A Beautiful Endeavour

SCENE ONE

I want to tell you a story. You might call it a love story. See what you make of it...

It concerns a local church that got into a conversation about same-sex attraction and following Jesus. It was lengthy, often animated and sometimes heated – yet remained, on the whole, respectful of the range of convictions and viewpoints held within the church.

It probably won't surprise you to learn that certain well known and often-quoted passages in the Bible were frequently visited – including those verses in the book of Leviticus (an ancient holiness code) where God's people, Israel, are told in no uncertain terms that it is an abomination for a man to lie with another man as he would with a woman, and that to do so warranted the death penalty for both parties.[6] Then there was the horrific tale of Sodom and Gomorrah.[7] The 'visit' to that infamous place was, to everybody's relief, short-lived. For most people, on all sides of the discussion, the threat of sexual violence by an angry mob, directed at two visitors to a town, had little bearing or light to shed on consensual, loving, same-sex relationships in our own setting.

Then there were the New Testament verses – from the writings of Saint Paul. I mean the two *vice lists* that include homosexual practice alongside greed, drunkenness, slander, swindling, murder, slave-trading and perjury; and the famous passage in Paul's letter to the Roman church, in which the rebellion of the Gentile (non-Jewish) world against its Creator is epitomised by women who exchange natural relations for unnatural, and men who burn with lust for one another.[8]

Some held that the obvious and clear meaning of these passages was that all same-sex sexual relations are clearly ruled out, though this was not to say (necessarily) that being same-sex attracted, in and of itself, was to be considered wrong or shameful.[9] Others argued, that the biblical writers were addressing forms of behaviour that were prevalent in their day. You may have heard of *pederasty*, where an adult male would have sex with a young lad in addition to normal marital relations with his wife; or of the temple cults where all kinds of perverse sexual rituals occurred. You will certainly be aware of the general degradation of Roman society, where all kinds of sexual excesses were practiced. The crux question for the church was whether the biblical passages were addressing these things only, or could be rightly applied to all same-sex relationships – even where they are characterised by committed love.

This part of the conversation went on for some time. I cannot give you all the details or nuances here. Suffice to say that no agreement was reached. However a turning point occurred when one of the older members of the church observed how limited the discussion had been so far, centring, as it had, on a handful of texts. He urged the church to widen its view: to progress the conversation within the Big Story of the Bible: from Creation through the Fall and Redemption to the New Creation.

It seemed like wise and timely counsel. So that is what they did...

SCENE TWO

Life's whole adventure was their canvas: from creation to rebellion to redemption to the renewal of all things.

The Garden of Eden seemed a good place to start. Whether history or allegory – and there were various views on that – all were agreed that profound and foundational truths were to be found there. God created us in his image. Magnificent creatures in an extravagant world, commissioned to rule over all this staggering beauty. Male and female he made us, two complimentary genders, made *one* in the gift and vocation of marriage, in which love may grow, children may be born and nurtured, and God's own self giving love made visible.

'It is a beautiful picture,' remarked Abigail. 'And yet it occurs to me that not all are called to partake in this kind of union. Not everyone finds a life-partner. Does that leave them in a lesser category?'

'Of course not,' replied Brett. 'Jesus wasn't married, nor was Paul, nor many other faithful disciples of Christ. In fact, the single life is much revered in Paul's writings. The marriage union between a man and a woman is not the only way in which God's nature and purpose is revealed.'

'So, what about a same-sex union?' That was Christine, chiming in. 'If two people of the same gender are attracted to each other – then I don't see why they can't form a loving bond in the same way as…'

'No, no! It doesn't work! I'm sorry…(Daniel looked apologetic for his interruption)… God made us male and female, and it's only in the joining of two different but complementary genders that a *one-flesh union* can occur.'[10]

Erica spoke up next. She wondered whether same-sex partners might complement each other in other ways: – 'like different personalities that fit together and make room for each other to grow.'

Farida felt this wasn't a good comparison – that gender differences were more fundamental than personality differences.

Graham argued that the complementarity of the sexes wasn't just 'a marriage thing,' but a gift for every human context – at home, in the workplace, in every sphere of life. 'I very much doubt that a few same-sex unions will upset the interplay of the sexes in the great scheme of things!'

Hadia wanted to get back to whether or not a loving same-sex union might be recognised as within God's creative purposes. 'As far as I can see, the one thing that can't happen is the natural conception of children. All the rest of what it means to be a couple seems possible: like companionship, friendship, and the love that grows within a committed, exclusive relationship – why not? Children can be nurtured too. I really can't see why such a love should be excluded.'

Ingrid responded, a little agitated: 'It just doesn't square with what we see in Eden, where God's purpose in creation is made abundantly clear. A man will leave his father and mother and be united to his wife…'[11]

'Still, we don't live in Eden, do we?' It was James' turn to speak. 'We have so far talked about God's purpose in his perfect creation – but that didn't last very long. We rebelled – God's magnificent image bearers were soon doing their own thing. Everything got broken. So, do we regard same-sex attraction as part of the brokenness of creation?

'Just typical!' retorted Kate. 'Anything or anyone that doesn't fit the norm gets put in a bin marked OUT OF ORDER – RESULT OF THE FALL.'

Liam came in at this point. 'Actually we are all in that bin, or boat – all of us are fallen, broken. Same-sex attraction is just one aspect of a disordered creation, one in a myriad of fallen features, all needing redemption in God's world. If we accept this, then the really important question is: *what will God do about it*? We believe in a God who acts to redeem his fallen creation – mending what is broken. So what does redemption look like for the same-sex attracted?

SCENE THREE

The idea of same-sex attraction as a sign of the fall was not accepted by everyone. Yet the question provoked by this view seemed worth pursuing. *What does redemption look like for the same-sex attracted? Or, what might it mean for a same-sex attracted person to follow Christ?*

Mary expressed her view that, whatever is broken, God can mend or heal. 'I believe that God can restore a person's sexuality as much as any other aspect of being human. What is more, I have a good friend for whom this is her testimony. She used to be attracted to other women – but was gloriously set free and is now dating men.'

'I know of other stories – not of healing, but of deep desperation and despair.' Nigel was visibly riled. 'I've a friend who tried for years to change his attractions. He got prayed for often, and some people even tried to deliver him – casting out the demons of homosexuality. He came close to ending his own life. He finally came to *accept* his sexuality.'[12]

'I see no problem with that,' remarked Oscar, 'provided he lives a celibate life. I've read moving accounts of those who embrace this call, and while it is not an easy road, it is a time-honoured path, and I believe that God's grace is poured out on those who take up their cross and walk in such costly obedience. The problem is often that churches are not always great at supporting people in that position – we are so well geared up for families, and yet can be really poor at loving and encouraging those who are single, *whatever* their sexuality.'

'My question,' responded Pat, 'is whether all gay people are necessarily called to celibacy. Maybe some are called to a loving, life-uniting relationship with someone they are attracted to and in love with. Marriage, as I understand it, is God's provision for our selfish desires to be schooled into self-giving love – a means of our redemption. When its work is done, it points to God's own love. Why can't a same-sex relationship be redemptive in the same way?'

'Because,' replied Quinn, 'the Bible gives no mandate for such a life-union. From Genesis to Revelation, marriage is a male-female union, and all sexual behaviour outside of that is regarded as immoral. It is not a popular message today, I know, but I can see no good reason to abandon what the Bible consistently teaches.'

Regina looked thoughtful. 'I accept that the Bible gives no alternative to male-female marriage, yet I wonder if the biblical writers could have conceived of such an alternative. Their understanding would have been that all same-sex behaviour reflected the perversion of natural desire. So the idea of same-sex attraction being natural to some – as we know today – would have been quite alien to them. Which means, I think, that we are considering a pattern of human life – committed, loving, same-sex relationships – that the Bible does not address directly. If I am right about this, then we need to turn to broader biblical themes – like truth, justice, mercy…'

'And inclusion,' offered Sam. 'I've been reading the Bible a lot since we began this, and one of things I have noticed is the way in which God keeps adding to his circle of friends. For example, there are rules early on in the history of Israel that excluded certain people from going to worship at the Temple, such as eunuchs and foreigners. Yet, later on in the great story of salvation, one of the prophets announces that eunuchs and foreigners will no longer be excluded, but will be given a name better than sons or daughters.[13] Much later on we see the way Jesus welcomes all the people on the margins of society. Later still, we see the amazement of the early Jewish disciples of Jesus as God opens the door to Gentile people – that's us I believe!'[14]

Tabitha responded. 'I get what you are driving at, but I think there is an important difference between Gentiles being welcomed into the church and the affirmation of same-sex relationships today. The salvation of the Gentiles was predicted in early times – right back to when Abraham received the promise that his offspring would be a blessing for all nations.[15] The promise is repeated throughout the Old Testament by psalmists and prophets. No such promise or prediction is made concerning the same-sex attracted.'

'Yes,' responded Ursula, 'but doesn't the church need to remain open to God's grace crossing more and more boundaries within human society, embracing those previously excluded – especially when we see people coming to faith? The fact of gay Christian couples today giving testimony to God's calling and blessing on their relationships must be reckoned with, surely.'

'So long as we don't just abandon the wisdom and judgement of previous generations of Christians in order to be acceptable to our society.' Now it was Vick's turn. 'We have a stable and consistent tradition on marriage and sexuality, held across centuries and continents: that marriage between a man and a woman is the only right context for sex. It's only in recent decades that other positions have been argued for, and only in the Western church, while the rest of the World church looks on in bemusement and concern.'

Xavier came in on this. 'I agree that our Christian tradition should be honoured – yet this doesn't mean it is beyond question or challenge. Over the centuries, some long-standing positions have shifted: such as our stance on slavery, attitudes to women in leadership, and our pastoral responses to those who are divorced and seek to re-marry, to name the obvious ones. The church in every generation has the responsibility to respond faithfully to the issues of its day, looking to the Spirit of God to guide us into all truth.'

'My fear,' responded Yvonne, 'is that we will be led more by our culture than by the Spirit of God…'

Well, the conversation ran on for many weeks, until it was somewhat interrupted by the appearance in the church of a same-sex couple, Shaz and Davina, along with their little boy, Zach.

Please note that alternative versions of Scenes Two and Three are given in Appendix 2 (pp. 38–44), prepared as scripts for four participants. Some have found this to be a more dynamic presentation, especially when reading aloud in a group context.

SCENE FOUR

Shaz and Davina attended an *Alpha* course run by the church – a ten-week course designed to introduce people to Jesus. They both came to faith and were filled with the Holy Spirit. They began to come along on Sunday mornings. They loved the warm and friendly atmosphere of the church, and their little boy, Zach, really enjoyed the Sunday school.[16]

One Sunday there was a service of Baptism, and Davina, deeply moved by the occasion, asked the pastor if she could meet him to talk about being baptised.

The pastor called in the following week for a chat over coffee – Shaz was there too. During the encounter, the pastor decided to be upfront with the couple about the conversation that was taking place in the church regarding same-sex attraction. Shaz asked if their presence was creating a problem: 'Is it okay for us to keep coming?' The pastor was at pains to reassure them they were most welcome, and said how good it was to see God working in their lives. But he also asked them for some time to reflect on Davina's request for baptism – which they agreed to.

The pastor met with his leaders over a number of weeks to consider the matter. They didn't actually talk much about sexuality – they talked mainly of baptism and *who* it was for.

Reading together through the book of Acts, which reports the earliest years of the church, they were struck by the way converts to the Christian faith were baptised immediately after their response to the gospel.[17] Those who received the good news were always headed straight for the water. Which challenged any idea that a person had to have everything sorted, or to reach a certain level of maturity in their faith, before baptism. Rather, baptism begins the journey.

'But what about repentance?' some were eager to ask. 'To turn to Christ involves turning from all that is wrong – surely Davina would need to give up her relationship with Shaz, or at least any sexual intimacy involved?' Not all agreed, reflecting the different views that had been expressed in the conversations of previous weeks. A number of the leaders were not so sure that the Bible prohibited all same-sex relationships and intimacy, and were inclined to give Shaz and Davina room to make their journey, trusting them to God's redeeming work. This idea grew as the leaders continued to talk. One of the leaders summed things up helpfully: 'These two women have come into a life-changing relationship with Jesus – let's trust them to God and see how he will lead them.'

So a baptism service was arranged.

As it turned out, both Shaz and Davina were baptised and later welcomed into membership of the church. The latter occasioned further discussion, but was carried by the shared conviction that since Shaz and Davina had been joined by God to Christ and to his church in baptism, there could be no good reason why this local church should not welcome them into its membership. In fact, it was reckoned to be the natural outworking of what God had done. Shaz and Davina became fully part of this fellowship of brothers and sisters in Christ, pledged to 'watch over each other and walk together' within the love and mission of Christ.[18]

SCENE FIVE

Shaz and Davina, and their little boy, continued to settle in to the life of the church. They joined a mid-week small group and began to help out with serving coffee on a Sunday morning, and setting up the Tuesday parent and toddlers group. Davina got involved in the worship band, and Shaz helped on the Alpha course. They made friends within the church, who brought a good deal of support and guidance to them in their fledgling faiths, helping them to work out what it meant to live in the way of Christ in all areas of their living. Zach enjoyed learning the stories of the Bible, and would tell them to his classmates in the playground – a budding evangelist it seemed!

In the main, the church was at peace about their three recent additions, but it has to be acknowledged that some were feeling less sure of things.

One member made an appointment to see the pastor to discuss his misgivings. 'Don't get me wrong, I love this couple and their little boy – he's a delight. It's just that, I wonder where this is all leading. It seemed so right to baptise them and to welcome them into membership, but I wonder and I worry about where this is going. I fear the slippery slope.'

'What do you mean exactly?' asked the pastor.

'Well,' replied the member, 'I am wondering what will happen if either Shaz or Davina shows leadership potential and gets nominated as a leader. What then? Or, what if we are approached to conduct a same-sex marriage – what then? That's what I mean by the slippery slope, Pastor.'

In time, both anticipations came about in the life of the church. Shaz turned out to be a born leader, and someone put her forward to be considered for the leadership team, which led to some deliberations. It was clear to the team that some in the church would be uneasy about such an appointment, and that to proceed could be divisive. In the end, it was Shaz who concluded that it would be unwise for her to stand – sensing the potential for tension within the church over this.

The request for marriage did not come from Shaz and Davina – who were in a civil partnership when they arrived at the church, and content with this as their way of pledging their commitment to each other and to Zach. It came from a male gay couple – Graham and Tony – who attended the church for a few months and then requested a church wedding. The pastor met them and, very courteously, declined to marry them. He explained that it was a matter of conscience for him personally, and that it would not be something the church community could do in unity. It was not received well, and news of the decision caused some consternation among some of the members, one of whom made an appointment to see the pastor and his wife.

'It's just not fair,' she exclaimed, not long after sitting down. Why can't we marry a same-sex couple? I don't get it. If they are committed to love each other "until death us do part"… it's just not fair! How is this just or loving?'

The pastor replied that his own understanding of what made a marriage would not allow him to conduct a gay wedding, and that such a course of action would almost definitely cause the church community to divide. He added that looking after the unity of the church was part of his calling: 'I know very well there are a number in the church who would make a case for a same-sex wedding or a formal blessing on a same-sex union. Yet for many in the church such actions would be betrayals of the Christian tradition that has guided us over many centuries. While our conversation continues, as it will for some time to come, we'll need to hold our tradition on marriage with care and caution, while seeking to be as loving and generous as we can to all whom God is bringing our way. That's what we've been working at, holding our differences well and giving room for people to grow in their relationship with Christ – honouring what God is doing in the lives of people like Shaz, Davina and Zach. Well, in all of us, really.'

There were some who left the church in the months that followed. Some went feeling that the church was not holding strongly enough to the traditional teachings of the church on same-sex relationships; others because the church had stopped short of a fully affirming position – especially in declining to marry a same-sex couple. The pastor was deeply grieved and made every effort to meet with those who signalled their intention to go, pleading with them to stay on the journey the church was making.

SCENE SIX

A few months on from the events I have related, the pastor was taking part in an ecumenical service at the Anglican church across the road. Something happened that he would never forget. It was at the part of the service where people are invited to come to the altar rail to take communion (the bread and wine that speak of Christ's body broken and his blood shed for us). He was moving towards the front and he could hardly believe his eyes as he saw the combination of people, in a line, kneeling at the altar rail. There was Shaz and Davina, and to their left was Jack, a young, gay, celibate man, who had been part of the church for several years. To their right was Jordan, a troubled young man who was earnestly seeking help to be free from same-sex desires. At either end of the line, like two bookends, *there* was Mr Slippery Slope, and *there* was Mrs It's Not Fair – each of them holding out their hands to receive the bread and wine of communion.

As the pastor arrived at the altar rail, now vacated, he fell to his knees and put out his hands to receive…

'The body of Christ broken for you… the blood of Christ shed for you… keep you in eternal life.'

And he wept.

SCENE SEVEN

There is one further happening that I must relate to you before I finish. It took place in the few seconds after the pastor reached the altar rail. Through his tears he had not noticed those who had joined him at his left and his right. On one side was Evelyn, the pastor of a church in a neighbouring village, on the other, Ian, also a local church leader. That three members from the local ministers fraternal should all arrive to take communion at once is not so remarkable, of course. Yet each of them knew what was represented in these moments.

Evelyn had been leading her church through a similar process to our pastor regarding same-sex attraction; so had Ian. The three communities had arrived at different positions. In Evelyn's church there had been a decision to re-affirm clearly the traditional view on same-sex relationships, though this had not happened without deep reflection, and recognition of the failure of our churches to love and receive those who are same-sex attracted. In Ian's church, the decision had been reached to embrace an affirming position towards LGBTQ+ people – again, not lightly taken, but the outcome of prolonged prayer and discussion. In both cases, those who held different views from the majority were strongly urged to remain within the church as brothers and sisters in Christ.

As for our pastor, in between his two friends and colleagues, well, you know quite a lot now about how things were in the community he led – of differences held in a loving tension, seeking to be faithful and generous together, making room for people to journey…

They held out their hands.

'The body of Christ broken for you… the blood of Christ, shed for you, Brother…

'The body of Christ broken for you... the blood of Christ shed for you, Sister.

'The body of Christ broken for you... the blood of Christ shed for you, Brother.'

Join the Conversation

If you have read the whole story in one continuous flow, take some time to gather your thoughts and reactions. It may help you to write these down. The following prompts and questions relate to each scene of the story in turn. You can use these to aid individual and/or group reflections.

SCENE ONE

A conversation begins.

1 Look up the passages referred to in this scene (see endnotes for Scene One). How do you react to them?

2 What do you make of the 'crux question' as to whether the passages are rightly applied to all same-sex relations or just certain forms prevalent in the contexts in which they were written?

You may be feeling that you would like to do some more reading or research on these passages. You could make a start by taking a look at Chapter Five in my book (Sexuality, Faith & the Art of Conversation – Part One), included in the sample chapters later in this book (pp. 57–70), which sets out both traditionalist and revisionist perspectives and arguments.

To help you explore these different perspectives further, I have suggested a variety of books and online resources in the resource section (pp. 29–30).

SCENE TWO

The church decides to widen their discussion beyond the 'condemning texts' and set it within the Big Story of the Scriptures. Most, if not all, who have written in this area have seen the wisdom of doing this – recognising that a position cannot be built on a handful of texts plucked out of the narrative of Scripture.

This scene seeks to indicate the various arguments being made in the wider conversation. These are broad-brush strokes, yet sufficient to give the essence of different approaches being taken today. The resources suggested at the end of the booklet will take you deeper in.

As mentioned earlier, a reworking of Scenes Two and Three is given in Appendix 2 (pp. 34–40), prepared as a script for four participants. Some have found this a more dynamic presentation, especially if you are reading aloud in a group context.

3 Read through the scene again. Notice/talk about which of the arguments make sense to you, and which you find less convincing. Do you find your thinking challenged by any of the contributions?

4 Take another look at Liam's claim at the end (p. 8). Is he right? Does his observation help the conversation forward?

SCENE THREE

Building on Liam's observation, the church pursues the question of what redemption might mean for the same-sex attracted.

5 Read through the scene again, following its development. Reflect on/discuss the various points made. As for Scene Two, consider what you find convincing/unconvincing and where your thinking is challenged.

6 Regina's comments (p. 10) touch on the place of reason in our ethical deliberations today. She suggests that our understanding today of same-sex attraction – informed by the scientific community – is different from that of the biblical writers, and that this will affect how we think about same-sex attraction and relationships today. What do you think about this?

It may be helpful at this point to take a look at Chapter Four of my book, Sexuality, Faith… Part One, included as a sample chapter later in this book (pp. 47–56), in which insights arising from biological and social studies are given some attention.

7 Vick points to a consistent tradition on same-sex relationships across centuries and continents (p. 11). Xavier counters that longstanding aspects of the Christian tradition (the accumulated wisdom of the church) have been challenged and changed over the centuries. Think about/discuss the place of tradition in navigating ethical issues today.

8 How do you respond to Yvonne's concern about the influence of cultural trends (p. 11)?

9 Take a look at the five summary viewpoints in Appendix 1 (pp. 31–33). Consider which of them is nearest to your view. You might find

you sit between two views. If you are in a group context, share where you each stand currently and let the conversation develop.

SCENE FOUR

The conversation of the church is somewhat interrupted by the appearance in the church of Shaz and Davina, and their little boy, Zach.

10 Read through the scene again. How well do you think the church responded to Shaz and Davina, and their little boy, in this scene?

11 What do you make of the leaders' reasoning and conclusion over baptism and membership for Davina and Shaz? For those in different church traditions – where baptism and belonging take different shape (e.g., infant baptism) – think about what equivalent conversations might take place.

12 Does the decision of the leaders to 'give room' to Shaz and Davina to work out their discipleship ring true for you?

Some who hold to a traditional view will see the baptism of Shaz and Davina, as well as their coming into membership, as examples of 'pastoral accommodation' – recognising that people come to Christ as they are, and that changes in lifestyle deemed consistent with following Christ may not be possible, or might take time. Such accommodation is regularly made in many churches in respect of those who remarry following divorce.

SCENE FIVE

Scene five tells of some concerns expressed within the church…

13 One member was worried about 'the slippery slope' and wondered what would happen if either Shaz or Davina was nominated for leadership in the church, or if a same-sex couple asked for a church wedding. Both anticipations came about. How well do you think the church handled them? What other issues might you imagine arising in this church? Do you think that such matters are best entrusted to the leadership team of a church?

14 Given the different understandings held in tension, how might the church in the story teach on Christian sexual morality – to children, teens and adults?[19]

15 Some members were offended at the refusal of the pastor to conduct a gay marriage, as voiced by the lady who came to visit him (Mrs It's Not Fair!). How do you feel the pastor handled this situation? Do you agree with his reasoning?

Many who are in same-sex relationships are not looking to marry, preferring a covenant relationship (civil partnership in the UK) or cohabitation. Some people have sought to make a biblical case for a same-sex covenant relationship – not claiming equivalence to heterosexual marriage, but seeing a loving bond of faithfulness that witnesses to God's love and purpose in a world that is broken.

16 Do you think that the church in our story might, in due course, be able to formally bless such a covenant relationship (as just described)? Do you think there is a good case for doing so?

17 Some people left the church for various reasons. Do you think that this might have been avoided, or is it inevitable?

SCENE SIX

The pastor weeps at the communion rail…

18 Reflect on/share your reactions to this short scene.

19 Where do your reactions take you?

A Beautiful Endeavour (the story) began life as a sermon illustration – quite a long one, around 15 minutes! In the original story, the conversation of the local church was first 'interrupted' by the appearance of a young man, Jordan, who it turned out was struggling with same-sex desires, looking for help and support to find freedom from them. Some months later, another young man, Jack, joined the church. He identified as gay and was exploring a call to celibacy. Later still, Shaz, Davina and Zach came into the church via an Alpha course. The story (in the sermon) explored pastoral responses to each of these life-situations, with different members of the church bringing friendship, wisdom and support as needed.

In Scene Six, all of these characters kneel at the altar rail together. I wanted to prompt some thinking about how a local church might hold its different viewpoints in a way that is good news for a variety of life-situations and commitments.

20 Do you think that a local church could embrace all three of the life-situations portrayed here, giving each one room to follow Christ and work out what this means for them?

21 Does holding a tension between different views on sexuality and faith help or hinder discipleship in the scenario sketched here? Is this missional or just a muddle?

SCENE SEVEN

Three pastors receive communion together…

22 Reflect on/share your reactions to this final scene.

23 Where do your reactions take you?

24 Can fellowship and unity be maintained between churches that reach different positions on sexuality and discipleship – especially within a union or network of churches? Think this one through for your particular tradition and circumstances.

NOTE FOR READERS IN BAPTIST CHURCHES

The Baptist Union of Great Britain (BUGB) Council has made two statements (2013 and 2016) to guide conversations within and between churches about human sexuality and same-sex relationships, and has sought to make the legal position of Baptist churches clear regarding the conducting of same-sex marriages (www.baptist.org.uk). This guidance and advice has been gathered and summarised in

Appendix 3: Guidance from the Wider Baptist Family' (pp. 41–44).

You will also find there a section of another statement issued in 2016, arising from an important conversation between a number of Baptist theologians and pastors holding a range of views on same-sex marriage, entitled **The Courage to Be Baptist: A Statement on Baptist Ecclesiology and Human Sexuality** (www.somethingtodeclare.org.uk).

RESOURCES FOR DELVING DEEPER

For a very thorough defence of the traditional view, you could look up Robert Gagnon's, *The Bible and Homosexual Practice*.[20] It's a weighty tome, but you can also access Gagnon's work via some video lectures at

http://www.walkingtogetherministries.com/2014/05/26/dr-robert-gagnons-videos-on-the-bible-and-homosexual-practice-at-skyline-church/.

A much more concise resource on the traditionalist side is the Evangelical Alliance's *Biblical and Pastoral Responses to Homosexuality*, edited by Andrew Goddard and Don Horrocks (London, 2012).

To gain a better understanding of the biblical and theological work under-pinning more affirming positions, you might take a look at Matthew Vines' *God and the Gay Christian*[21] or James Brownson's, *Bible, Sexuality and Gender*.[22] If video works best for you, check out a series of short talks by Andrew Tallon, who is Tutor for Biblical Studies at Northern Baptist College, http://www.bibleandhomosexuality.org/.

For an excellent discussion of contrasting views and approaches, try *Two Views on Homosexuality, the Bible and the Church*, edited by Preston Sprinkle.[23] Reading it, I was thoroughly impressed by the quality and tone of the contributions, and the interaction between the authors. It was such a stimulating and heartening read – a conversation rather than a treatise.

For a compassionate, thoughtful pastoral response that arises from a deep engagement with LGBTQ+ people, get hold of Andrew Marin's *Love is an Orientation*.[24]

29

For autobiographies, I recommend reading and comparing Wesley Hill's, *Washed and Waiting*,[25] and Vicky Beeching's, *Undivided*.[26]

Finally, my own book, *Sexuality, Faith & the Art of Conversation – Part One*, explores how the conversation about same-sex attraction and following Jesus might be pursued with integrity and kindness, weaving together original research, stories, essays and fictional conversations set in the Wild Goose Coffee Shop. One reviewer described the book as

> … a model of biblically faithful, pastorally involved engagement that points a way forward not only on this issue but on many others.[27]

Parts Two, Three & Four (one volume) are now also available, the introduction to which is included on pp. 71–72 of this book.

APPENDIX 1:

FIVE CHRISTIAN VIEWS ON SAME-SEX RELATIONSHIPS

The following began as four viewpoints included in the resources of the Baptist Union Working Group on Human Sexuality. I have developed them, adding a fifth view (D) and extending view E to include Gay Marriage as a possible outcome of its reasoning.

A Scripture condemns all homosexual practice, and the church should always regard it as sinful. Furthermore, same-sex attraction should be repented of and healing sought from such desires. It is contradictory to speak of being a 'gay Christian', since the path to holiness must involve the transformation of disordered sexuality within a loving Christian community.

B Scripture clearly denounces same-sex sexual acts, but says nothing about sexual orientation. A distinction must be made between orientation and practice, otherwise those who experience same-sex desires will conclude that their temptations make them unacceptable to God, which is against the grain of biblical truth. A celibate homosexual is no more sinful than a celibate heterosexual, both of whom must learn restraint and seek to live a life of purity. However, it may be that within the loving and prayerful support of a Christian community, someone with a same-sex orientation can experience healing (a change of orientation), opening up the possibility of (heterosexual) marriage.

C Scripture's condemnation of same-sex sexual behaviour seems to have in view unloving acts that exploit others and/or involve the perversion of sexual desire. These include gang rape, pederasty, temple prostitution and the search by heterosexuals for illicit sexual thrills. It is difficult, therefore, to make a decision about the acceptability of a loving, exclusive, same-sex partnership from the few biblical texts that make reference to same-sex acts directly. However, the biblical norm from Creation onwards is marriage between a man and a woman, and no alternative is envisaged apart from celibacy, which is given high status in the writings of Paul in the New Testament. Celibacy, for both homosexuals and heterosexuals, therefore, needs to be recovered as a high calling, and re-valued by the church community over and against a culture that sees sexual fulfilment as a right and a necessity.

At the same time, great care should be taken to avoid putting pressure on those who are same-sex attracted to seek and experience change in their sexual orientation, as this typically brings more feelings of guilt than healing. As for the idea that a good heterosexual marriage will bring about the needed change, there are many casualties that say otherwise.

D While the Bible's references to same-sex sexual practice most likely refer to behaviour that is unloving and exploitative, the creation narratives make it clear that God's original purpose held no alternative beyond male-female marriage, except celibacy (by implication and developed in later parts of Scripture). However, the fall of mankind brought disorder and brokenness to creation, and same-sex attraction is only one example of this. Since we believe in a God who acts constantly to redeem his fallen creation, it is important to ask how he might work with those who are strongly same-sex attracted and unlikely to change in their sexual orientation. We experience God working to transform our brokenness in many creative ways. Could a loving, committed, same-sex partnership be one of those ways, even if not within the original purpose of creation?

E The condemnations in Scripture of same-sex sexual practice are aimed at unloving, exploitative acts, and no prohibition is found concerning loving, committed same-sex relationships. What Scripture everywhere affirms is covenant loyalty, and this is given its clearest affirmation in marriage (between a man and a woman). However, it can also be expressed in faithful, loving and monogamous same-sex partnerships between people of pronounced same-sex orientation, and such are worthy of the blessing of the church as an expression of God's purpose for human community, which is loving and committed human relationship.

Among those who hold viewpoint E, there are different outlooks on Gay Marriage. Some are affirming, while others – including some who are same-sex attracted – point to the blessing of a covenant commitment (such as civil partnership in the UK) as more fitting.

APPENDIX 2:

ALTERNATIVE SCRIPTS FOR SCENES TWO & THREE (FOUR VOICES)

SCENE TWO

NARRATOR: The Garden of Eden seemed a good place to start. Whether history or allegory -- and there were various views on that -- all were agreed that profound and timeless truths were to be found there. God created us in his image. Magnificent creatures in an extravagant world, commissioned to rule over all this staggering beauty. Male and female he made us, two complimentary genders, made one in the gift and vocation of marriage, in which love may grow, children may be born and nurtured, and God's own, self-giving love made visible.

ASHLEY: It is a beautiful picture. And yet it occurs to me that not all are called to partake in this kind of union. Not everyone finds a life-partner. Does that leave them in a lesser category?

BROOK: Of course not! Jesus wasn't married, nor was Paul, nor many other faithful disciples of Christ. In fact, the single life is much revered in Paul's writings. The marriage union between a man and a woman is not the only way in which God's nature and purpose is revealed.

ASHLEY: So, what about a same-sex union? If two people of the same gender are attracted to each other – then I don't see why they can't form a loving bond in the same way as…

BROOK: No, no! It doesn't work! I'm sorry…(looking apologetic for the interruption)… God made us male and female, and it's only in the joining of two different but complementary genders that a *one-flesh union* can occur.[1]

ASHLEY: Yes, but I wonder if same-sex partners might complement each other in other ways – like different personalities that fit together and make room for each other to grow.

CHRIS: I don't think that's good comparison – gender differences are more fundamental than personality differences.

DREW: Can I just say that, in my mind, complementarity of the sexes isn't just 'a marriage thing,' but a gift for every human context – at home, in the workplace, in every sphere of life. I very much doubt that a few same-sex unions will upset the interplay of the sexes in the great scheme of things!

ASHLEY: I'd like to get back to whether or not a loving same-sex union might be recognised as within God's creative purposes. As far as I can see, the one thing that can't happen is the natural conception of children. All the rest of what it means to be a couple seems possible: like companionship, friendship, and the love that grows within a committed, exclusive relationship – why not? Children can be nurtured too. I really can't see why such a love should be excluded.

CHRIS: It just doesn't square with what we see in Eden, where God's purpose in creation is made abundantly clear. A man will leave his father and mother and be united to his wife…[2]

DREW: Still, we don't live in Eden, do we? We have so far talked about God's purpose in his perfect creation – but that didn't last very long.

---

1 Genesis 2:24, Mark 10:8.
2 Genesis 2:24, Mark 10:8.

We rebelled – God's magnificent image bearers were soon doing their own thing. Everything got broken. So, do we regard same-sex attraction as part of the brokenness of creation?

ASHLEY: Just typical! Anything or anyone that doesn't fit the norm gets put in a bin marked **OUT OF ORDER – RESULT OF THE FALL.**

DREW: Actually we are all in that bin, or boat – all of us are fallen, broken. Same-sex attraction is just one aspect of a disordered creation, one in a myriad of fallen features, all needing redemption in God's world. If we accept this, then the really important question is: *what will God do about it?* We believe in a God who acts to redeem his fallen creation – mending what is broken. So what does redemption look like for the same-sex attracted?'

SCENE THREE (ALTERNATIVE)

NARRATOR: The idea of same-sex attraction as a sign of the fall was not accepted by everyone. Yet the question provoked by this view seemed worth pursuing. *What does redemption look like for the same-sex attracted? Or, what might it mean for a same-sex attracted person to follow Christ?*

CHRIS: The way I see it, whatever is broken, God can mend or heal. I believe that God can restore a person's sexuality as much as any other aspect of being human. What is more, I have a good friend for whom this is her testimony. She used to be attracted to other women – but was gloriously set free, and is now dating men.

DREW: Well I know of other stories – not of healing, but of deep desperation and despair. I've a friend who tried for years to change his attractions. He got prayed for often, and some people even tried to deliver him – casting out the 'demons of homosexuality'. He came close to ending his own life. He finally came to *accept* his sexuality.

BROOK: I see no problem with that, provided he lives a celibate life. I've read moving accounts of those who embrace this call, and while it is not an easy road, it is time-honoured path, and I believe that God's grace is poured out on those who take up their cross and walk in such costly obedience. The problem is often that churches are not always great at supporting people in that position – we are so well geared up for families, and yet can be really poor at loving and encouraging those who are single, *whatever* their sexuality.

ASHLEY: My question is whether all gay people are necessarily called to celibacy. Maybe some are called to a loving, life-uniting relationship with someone they are attracted to and in love with. Marriage, as I understand it, is God's provision for our selfish desires to be schooled into self-giving love – a means of our redemption. When its work is done, it points to God's own love. Why can't a same-sex relationship be redemptive in the same way?

BROOK: Because the Bible gives no mandate for such a life-union. From Genesis to Revelation, marriage is a male-female union and all sexual behaviour outside of that is regarded as immoral. It is not a popular message today, I know, but I can see no good reason to abandon what the Bible consistently teaches.'

DREW: I accept that the Bible gives no alternative to male-female marriage, yet I wonder if the biblical writers could have conceived of such an alternative. Their understanding would have been that all same-sex behaviour reflected the perversion of natural desire. So the idea of same-sex attraction being natural to some – as we know today – would have been quite alien to them. Which means, I think, that we are considering a pattern of human life – committed, loving, same-sex relationships – that the Bible does not address directly. If I am right about this, then we need to turn to broader biblical themes – like truth, justice, mercy…'

ASHLEY: And inclusion! I've been reading the Bible a lot since we began this, and one of things I have noticed is the way in which God keeps adding to his circle of friends. For example, there are rules early on in the history of Israel that excluded certain people from going to worship at the Temple, such as eunuchs and foreigners. Yet, later on in the great story of salvation, one of the prophets announces that eunuchs and foreigners will no longer be excluded, but will be given a name better than sons or daughters.[3] Much later on we see the way Jesus welcomes all the people on the margins of society. Later still, we see the amazement of the early Jewish disciples of Jesus as God opens the door to Gentile people – that's us I believe!'[4]

---

3 Isaiah 56:3-8.
4 Acts 11:1-18.

CHRIS: I get what you are driving at, but I think there is an important difference between Gentiles being welcomed into the church and the affirmation of same-sex relationships today. The salvation of the Gentiles was predicted in early times – right back to when Abraham received the promise that his offspring would be a blessing for all nations.[5] The promise is repeated throughout the Old Testament by psalmists and prophets. No such promise or prediction is made concerning the same-sex attracted.'

ASHLEY: Yes, but doesn't the church need to remain open to God's grace crossing more and more boundaries within human society, embracing those previously excluded – especially when we see people coming to faith? The fact of gay Christian couples today giving testimony to God's calling and blessing on their relationships must be reckoned with, surely.

BROOK: So long as we don't just abandon the wisdom and judgement of previous generations of Christians in order to be acceptable to our society. We have a stable and consistent tradition on marriage and sexuality, held across centuries and continents: that marriage between a man and a woman is the only right context for sex. It's only in recent decades that other positions have been argued for, and only in the Western church, while the rest of the World church looks on in bemusement and concern.

DREW: I agree that our Christian tradition should be honoured – yet this doesn't mean it is beyond question or challenge. Over the centuries, some long-standing positions have shifted: such as our stance on slavery, attitudes to women in leadership, and our pastoral responses to those who are divorced and seek to re-marry, to name the obvious ones. The church in every generation has the responsibility to respond faithfully to the issues of its day, looking to the Spirit of God to guide us into all truth...

---

5 Genesis 12:1-3.

CHRIS: My fear is that we will be more led by our culture than by the Spirit of God…

BROOK: I agree, we live in an age where truth is relative and anything goes. Everyone gets to decide their own values – our young people have never been in such peril…

CHRIS: We need to return to our moorings – get back to the true freedom story of our Christian heritage…

NARRATOR: (cutting in) Well, the conversation ran on for many weeks, until it was somewhat interrupted by the appearance in the church of a same-sex couple, Shaz and Davina, along with their little boy, Zach.

APPENDIX 3

GUIDANCE FROM THE WIDER BAPTIST FAMILY

OUR LEGAL POSITION

Following the Same Sex Marriage Bill of 2013, the Baptist Union of Great Britain (BUGB) Council sought to make clear the implications of the bill to our Baptist churches, including

- Baptists do not conduct marriage ceremonies under the same part of the legislation as the established church (Church of England). Baptists have never had, and will never have, an obligation to provide marriage services in the same way that the established church does.
- Under the provision of the 2013 Act a religious organisation that wishes to conduct a same sex marriage must **re-register** their building. The current licence is not sufficient; **a church will have to make a conscious decision to opt-in**.
- The government continues to say that no minister and/or individual church will be forced to conduct a same sex marriage. This is protected in law, with provision in the Equality Act for refusal on religious conscience.

BAPTIST UNION (BUGB) COUNCIL STATEMENTS

Emerging from a listening process across our denomination and much reflection, the BUGB Council has made two statements about same-sex relationships and marriage. Both point to our first principle of declaration: *That our Lord and Saviour Jesus Christ, God manifest in the flesh, is the sole and absolute authority in all matters pertaining to faith and practice, as revealed in the Holy Scriptures, and that each church has liberty, under the guidance of the Holy Spirit, to interpret and administer His Laws.* Accordingly, the May 2014 statement affirms the liberty of a local church 'to determine its own mind of this matter… recognising the freedom of a minister to respond to the wishes of their church meeting, where their conscience permits, without breach of disciplinary guidelines.' At the same time, the same statement affirms the traditionally accepted Biblical understanding of Christian marriage, as a union between a man and a woman, and makes it clear that a Baptist minister in a sexual relationship outside of marriage (as just defined), would be in breach of their ministerial vows and their actions deemed conduct unbecoming (gross misconduct).

Two years later, in March 2016, Council issued the following.

BAPTISTS TOGETHER AND REGISTRATION OF OUR BUILDINGS FOR SAME-SEX MARRIAGE

Biblical Marriage Re-affirmed – Council positively re-affirms and commends to our churches our Union's historic biblical understanding of marriage as a union between one man and one woman, and calls them to live in the light of it.

This is a response to the introduction of The Marriage (Same Sex Couples) Act 2013, and churches seeking clarification of the BUGB response to the matter of registering buildings for the solemnisation of same-sex marriage.

This understanding has shaped the rules for accredited Baptist ministers regarding sexuality and the ministry and our rules continue to remain unchanged (see www.baptist.org.uk/minrecrules).

Baptist Ecclesiology – The Declaration of Principle, which is the basis of our Union, states: *'That our Lord and Saviour Jesus Christ…'* (see in full, p. 43).

This way of being church stresses our unity as disciples of our 'Lord and Saviour Jesus Christ,' and acknowledges the potential for some diversity in pastoral and missional practice. As disciples covenanting together in humility we seek God's help to live with the tension of our independence and interdependence as Baptist churches.

Called to Mission – The Declaration of Principle also states: *'That it is the duty of every disciple to bear personal witness to the Gospel of Jesus Christ, and to take part in the evangelisation of the world.'*

Therefore, as a gospel people we renew our commitment to engaging in sharing the good news with all people and encourage our churches to reach out to every part of their communities with imagination and compassion.

Walking together in Unity – Reflecting on the issue of churches registering their buildings for same-sex marriage, Council recognises areas of genuine and deep disagreement. We believe that these are dimensions of the tension of living with unity and diversity. We continue to seek God's grace as we 'walk together and watch over one another' under the authority of Christ.

In the light of this, recognising the costs involved and after careful and prayerful reflection and listening, we humbly urge churches who are considering conducting same-sex marriages to refrain from doing so out of mutual respect. At the same time, we also humbly urge all churches to remain committed to our Union out of mutual respect; trusting that the One who unites us is stronger than what divides us.

SOMETHING TO DECLARE: THE COURAGE TO BE BAPTIST

During 2016, a group of Baptist theologians and pastors, holding between them a range of convictions and viewpoints on same-sex marriage, met to discuss the matter. The fruit of their engagement, published in December of 2016, includes the following:

'What, then, shall we do?' The authors of this statement believe that the courageous and truly faithful response is to trust that the ways we believe God has called us to live together are adequate to this present crisis.

- We call for local churches to engage together much more deeply and honestly than before, so that we truly know and are known.
- We call for serious, open-ended, and respectful conversation, directed towards enriching our shared mission: this is our 'conversation waiting to begin'.
- We call for shared trust and good faith, a commitment to believe that those churches with whom we disagree take their positions out of a desire to shape life according to the gospel, and to follow faithfully the laws of Christ disclosed in Scripture.
- We call for a willingness to allow every church to follow its own discernment of Christ's call on its life, and a willingness on the part of every church to allow its discernment to be questioned and challenged by others.
- We call, rather simply, for Baptist churches to have the courage to be Baptist.

We do not pretend that this will be easy. It will be costly. It will take time and effort that could be given elsewhere. It will involve our churches making themselves vulnerable at deep points. It will require churches to live with tensions and disagreements that some will find close to unbearable. We believe, however, that however protracted, painful, and precarious this existence might be, it is in fact our only place of true safety and security, because it is the place where God is calling us to live.

There will be churches amongst us who believe the demands of justice for LGBT+ people are so urgent that they will wish to resist this call to conversation and co-existence; there will be other churches who believe their own contextual mission will be so compromised by any re-examination of marriage that they will also want to resist. We call both sets of churches to have patience with those churches that are not yet so certain, to walk with them and help them to know better Christ's ways, despite the cost that comes with such patience.

There may be other churches on either side who will be uninterested in further conversation because they cannot imagine how a position other than their own could be faithful or biblical. To such we say, gently but seriously, that the limits of your—or our—imagination are not a good source of theological insight. The gospel call remains to be transformed by the renewing of our minds, to discover that sometimes, often, God gives more than we can imagine. The smallness of our imaginations can never be a reason to denigrate God's gifts.

Amongst the authors of this statement are some who believe that a properly Baptist engagement over sexual ethics will lead our churches to re-assert that male-female marriage is the only Christian way and others who believe that it will lead our churches to embrace same-sex marriage as a profoundly Christian option. We talk about these things in private, and (some of us) in very public spaces too. We do not expect to convince each other any time soon, but in maintaining our friendships, learning from each other, and discovering more of the missional contexts and biblical insights that make us advocates for our differing positions, we encourage each other to follow Christ more faithfully even as we disagree. This, we believe, is our Baptist way.

Sources:
https://www.baptist.org.uk/Groups/273782/Human_Sexuality.aspx.
http://www.somethingtodeclare.org.uk/.

SEXUALITY, FAITH & THE ART OF CONVERSATION

– PART ONE –

SAMPLE CHAPTERS

CHAPTER 4

First Gathering (Session One)

Church Youth Lounge: Saturday, 15 February 2014 – 9:00 to 13:00

Present: Steve, Greta, Richard, Lewis, Chris, Maureen, Abigail, Patrick, James and Dru
Absent: Erica and Monica

The first meeting of the group was a whole morning together. The purpose of this session was to allow Steve to take the group through the Baptist Union materials, 'Baptists Exploring Issues of Homosexuality',[28] as a way into the conversation and to help us get our bearings for the months ahead.

After a short time of worship, we took time to introduce ourselves and to share how we were each feeling. A number within the group spoke of feeling 'torn': desiring to welcome and include those who are homosexual without judging, and yet anxious that the Bible's teaching on same-sex behaviour did not seem to allow this. Some spoke of a 'head and heart' divergence – usually meaning that their head said 'no', following the biblical prohibitions, while their heart said 'yes' to being inclusive. A good number expressed the sense of relief and liberation at being able to talk about a subject that is often avoided in church.

Steve went on to remind everyone of the task we were taking on together: *to craft a pastoral response to those who live with same-sex desires and seek to follow Christ*, to be submitted to the church meeting in July of 2014. He then set out a proposed approach to the task. Essentially, Steve called the group to a conversation befitting our shared commitment to follow Christ and reflecting our Baptist heritage. This was to include a commitment to the Christian Scriptures as our primary text, depending on the Holy Spirit to guide us into truth – as articulated in the first principle of the Baptist Union.[29] We took some time to get the measure of this statement and to consider how we might enact it in our conversation together. This involved a discussion of what constituted a good theological conversation, including attention to what might be termed our Big Story – moving from Creation to Fall to Redemption to New Creation.[30] It also included the key theological question, 'What kind of God does Scripture reveal?' – recognising that our answers to this question will significantly shape our understanding of what it means to live faithfully towards him. We agreed upon complementary approaches to listening to what Scripture is saying to us today: sometimes working from the text to the world; while at other times the other way around. The group also agreed on some principles concerning the integrity and quality of our interactions: such as being aware of how we are shaped by our own individual backgrounds, as well as the culture we share. We agreed upon practicing mutual respect, seeking to listen well and, above all, letting love inform and guide our conversation.

Having agreed these general principles, the group decided upon the following specific protocols:

- We are aiming for a space to explore ideas and feelings without fear of being judged. Sometimes one or other may want to try out an idea that is tentative, and we want to encourage this.
- We desire for the group to be supportive of one another – sometimes it might be helpful for one of us to seek out another group member to talk over how the conversations we are having are impacting them.
- We are free to share our own views with others outside the group (being wise) but not the views of other group members.

- It's fine to talk with others (outside the group) about how the group is getting on in general terms – bearing in mind that they will not have the same support we have in working these issues through (be wise and caring).

Having reached agreements on the approach of our conversation and some specific protocols, we proceeded to the materials provided by the Baptist Union (BU) working group.

SCIENCE, STATISTICS AND THE SPIRIT OF THE AGE

Steve gave a brief overview of the various kinds of research into the causes of homosexuality… [31] He offered a caution about oversimplifications: such as the idea of a 'gay-gene'[32] determining that some people are homosexual, or the 'one size fits all' approach that puts all occurrences of same-sex attraction down to relationships with parents – so, for example, male homosexuality has commonly been associated with an absent father (whether physically or emotionally) and/or a dominant mother.

The group found the materials both stimulating and perplexing. There was no clear conclusion to be reached on causation, except the likelihood of a combination of genetic disposition, environmental factors and personal choice in determining sexual orientation, identity and lifestyle. However, it did occur to the group that whatever the balance of factors at play, it was important to recognise that a small minority of people experience same-sex attraction as a 'given', with little likelihood of change. So that perhaps the most pertinent issue is not causation, but how we respond to people as they are.

FOCUS: On Causation and Change[33]

Those who have reviewed the various studies looking into the causes of homosexuality have tended to arrive at what might be called 'integrative theories'. Keener and Swartzendruber, for example, conclude, 'It is impossible to neatly separate our heredity from our environment; both are important determinants in the person we have become.'[34] Jones and Yarhouse concur, and have reflected helpfully on the popular assumptions that genetic causation is firmly established and psychological studies largely discredited.[35] On the basis of their investigations, they assert that biological theories are far from conclusive and that psychological theories are far from being disproved.[36]

Francis Collins, the leader of the Human Genome Project, offers a perspective on the relative contributions of genetic and other factors, with reference to a specific area of research:

> Evidence from twin studies does in fact support the conclusion that heritable factors play a role in male homosexuality. However, the likelihood that the identical twin of a homosexual male will also be gay is about 20% (compared with 2-4 percent of males in the general population), indicating that sexual orientation is genetically influenced but not hardwired by DNA, and that whatever genes are involved represent predispositions, not predeterminations.[37]

This verdict is supported by a recent report on a wide survey of scientific studies, which concludes that 'The understanding of sexual orientation as an innate, biological fixed property of human beings – the idea that people are "born that way" – is not supported by scientific evidence.'[38] The writers go on to say that 'While there is evidence that biological factors such as genes and hormones are associated with sexual behaviours and attractions, there are no compelling causal biological explanations for human sexual orientation.'[39]

If we accept the likely interplay of genetic, environmental, and other factors (including personal choice) in forming sexuality and its expression – though presumably differing from person to person – this might seem to suggest that a change of orientation is a reasonable pursuit for someone who is same-sex attracted. (Though we would do well to heed the caution of Collins that the fact of non-genetic influences does not imply that these are inherently alterable.[40])

Leanne Payne, a Christian Counsellor and author, focuses on emotional and psychological factors in a therapeutic approach to helping people find freedom from homosexual desires – viewing such desires as symptoms of emotionally deficient relationships and/or traumatic experiences in childhood.[41] Some of Payne's case studies centre on experiences of past abuses that have led to a broken or repressed masculinity or femininity. Others focus more on the deficit left in a person's development by their growing up with an absent parent (whether physically or emotionally) or someone who dominates or controls them. Whatever the relational or situational root, Payne confidently advocates a journey of healing that seeks to address what is broken and help the individual towards a restored sexuality. This is a loving, gentle and prayerful process.

In 'Exchanging the Truth of God for a Lie', Jeremy Marks cites Payne as one of the inspirations for the ministry of 'Courage'[42], an organisation set up by Marks in February 1988 to offer support to those living with same-sex desires to live celibate lives and, as the ministry developed in confidence, to move on from homosexual orientation. In his book, Marks describes how the ministry initially burgeoned, moving from weekly support groups to the provision of a one-year residential discipleship course that provided a strong community life as a context for overcoming homosexual desires. However, there came a point when Marks began to feel uneasy and unsure about the long term fruit of the ministry, as he discovered that an alarming number of former community members did not continue to experience the freedom they had found in the community: with many becoming depressed or finding a greater sense of release and freedom in accepting their homosexual orientation. Shaken by the seeming ineffectiveness of the healing ministry for those who were homosexual, and the apparent ill-effects of insisting on celibacy for those who could not change, Marks led an 'about-turn' [43] and committed *Courage* to supporting gay Christians in their life-style choices, whether that be celibacy, a committed, loving (sexual) relationship with someone of the same sex, or continuing within a gay/straight marriage.

Therapies aimed at changing a person's sexual orientation have long been regarded as suspect within medical circles and general society – which no doubt explains the lack of recent research in this area.[44] Jones and Yarhouse reviewed the success rates of change therapies carried out in the 1950s, 1960s and 1970s. They comment that most of these were methodologically weak – particularly in the way outcomes were measured – to the extent that their results are usually deemed unreliable. However, looking across a wide range of studies, Jones and Yarhouse offer an average positive outcome of 33%.[45] It is important to note that this estimate includes a range of behaviour modifications and impulse changes that do not constitute a change of orientation. It appears that while there may be some evidence of radical change, it is rare.[46]

As already intimated, encouraging a person towards a change of sexual orientation is increasingly viewed as unethical and potentially harmful, particularly by medical authorities.[47] Churches and ministries that guide and support people in this way have courted a lot of criticism. Yet, if a person's sexuality and its expression emerge from a complex interaction of genetic, environmental and experiential factors, then I would venture that loving and prayerful attention to a psychological or emotional wound – such as that caused by some form of abuse or neglect – may be appropriate for some people, provided it is sought after and not imposed. In such cases there should not be any pressure towards a change that many have found elusive. Equally, and by the same logic – recognising a complex interaction of factors and the uniqueness of each person's formation – the assumption of a relational or traumatic root for same-sex attraction would be misplaced for others, and such counselling or ministry inappropriate.

GROUP SESSION ONE CONTINUED

Following the brief tour of scientific investigations into causation and change, the working group considered sociological research into the statistical incidence of same-sex orientation and behaviour. This began with the famous work of Alfred Kinsey, carried out in the 1940s and 1950s, which was built on the idea of sexual experience as a continuum ranging from exclusively heterosexual to exclusively homosexual, with all gradations in between. (It was Kinsey's work that gave us the familiar and often quoted '1 in 10' statistic for male homosexuality.) Steve referred to more recent studies, such as the first National Survey of Sexual Attitudes and Lifestyles (Natsal 1), 1990, which reported that around 1% of men and 0.5% of women were same-sex attracted, with the percentage for actual sexual experience being the same for men and a little lower (0.3%) for women.[48] These results came as something of surprise for most members of the group.

The disparity between Kinsey's '1 in 10' and the more recent statistics led us to consider the highly politicised nature of the same-sex issue and the lack of nuance given in media portrayals of viewpoints held. The point was made that those who hold a view that is not wholly accepting of the choices made by those who live with same-sex desires can easily be branded 'homo-phobic', even when the middle ground is held with careful thought and compassion. We agreed that part of our task was to resist such pressure, along with pressure from the other end of the spectrum, where even entering into such a conversation as ours might quickly be seen as suspect or unfaithful towards what the Bible clearly teaches (within a traditional viewpoint).

FOCUS: ON MEASURING SEXUALITY

The Natsal 1 survey referenced above is over twenty years old. Understandably the group were keen to learn if more recent studies showed significant change. A much more recent survey conducted for the Office of National Statistics between January and December of 2012 indicated percentages of men and women identifying as gay or lesbian at 1.5% and 0.7% respectively – suggesting little change over two decades.[49] Newspapers reporting on these results, including the Guardian and the Daily Mail, reflected on the disparity between Kinsey's '1 in 10' and the ONS data, and rehearsed the usual criticisms of Kinsey's methods – such as the non-random selection of interviewees – but went on to question whether persistent taboos around sexual identity continue to inhibit disclosure of sexual orientation. Supporting this suspicion, Rose Everleth, writing for the Smithsonian, reports on a new study in America that has returned higher proportions than usual of those identifying as gay or lesbian, and observes that this seems to be due to the use of 'veiled' questions.[50]

Whether or not the proportions of those identifying as gay or lesbian are understated, they hardly tell the whole story of sexual diversity in Britain, or indeed America. This can be demonstrated by looking at some other measures of sexuality reported in the Natsal surveys of 1990, 2000 and 2010, as shown in the table below.

Sexual practices with partners of the same sex[51]	Men			Women		
	N1	*N2*	*N3*	*N1*	*N2*	*N3*
Any sexual experience or contact with partner of the same sex	6.0%	8.4%	7.3%	3.7%	9.7%	16.0%
Any sexual experience with genital contact with partner of the same sex	3.6%	5.4%	4.8%	1.8%	4.0%	7.9%
At least one sexual partner of the same sex in the past 5 years	1.5%	2.5%	2.9%	0.8%	2.4%	4.7%

These percentages show that beyond those who identify as gay, lesbian or bi-sexual, there are considerably more who disclose some degree of same-sex experience, with the overall trend from Natsal 1 to Natsal 3 being upward. A closer look at the Natsal 3 statistics reveals a higher level of same-sex sexual activity among younger age-groups and a more fluid sexuality among females – the last point strikingly indicated in the grid above with 16% of women reporting some kind of same-sex contact or experience.

In the face of such data, it is important to distinguish those who are gay or bisexual, and in committed relationships, from those who are experimenting with same-sex intimacy in an increasingly permissive society (if it feels good…). For the latter, we might see a more obvious application of the so called condemning texts, than for those of pronounced homosexual orientation who live in faithful, long term relationships. This will clearly depend on how these texts are interpreted: whether they are aimed only at sexual behaviour that is lustful and exploitative or experimental or divorced from long-term loving relationship – or if they have a wider reference and application.

To these texts and the broader perspective of the Bible, the working group turned its attention next.

CHAPTER FIVE

What the Bible Has to Say

GROUP SESSION ONE CONTINUED

Before looking together at the texts that make reference to same-sex behaviour, Steve proposed some preliminary agreements (shared understandings of the biblical perspective on human sexuality and its expression) on which we might build our discussions:

- Promiscuous and exploitative sex is wrong – whether homosexual or heterosexual.
- Scripture affirms marriage between male and female as the creational intention/norm.
- God is a God of covenant relationship, reflected in loving, faithful relationships: including marriage, friendship, the care of children, etc.

The group had no difficulty in agreeing to these and also confirmed that the question before us was not about whether any kind of same-sex behaviour might be acceptable, but specifically that within a loving, committed, life partnership between two people of the same sex.

From here, a few more points were offered and agreed relating to the specific texts to be considered:

- There are few texts that deal directly with homosexuality and all of them are disapproving.

- In the ancient world there was no distinction between 'sexual orientation' and 'sexual practice'.
- A key question is whether these texts address all homosexual behaviour or certain forms prevalent in the ancient world, e.g., pederasty.

The first of these was accepted as self-evident. The second was received as helpful in avoiding the projection of this relatively modern way of thinking onto the ancient text. The third was to become a familiar friend, for in all our discussions of the *condemning texts* we kept coming back to the question: 'What is being addressed here?'

So our first consideration (as a working group) of our key-texts began. We read them together, and Steve outlined both traditional and revisionist understandings of each text to provoke and facilitate the discussion. This took the remainder of our time – so that we had to agree at the end to pick up the other main session envisaged (responding to stories) at our next meeting.

By the end of our time, the pertinence of the key question (what is being forbidden and condemned?) was clear to everyone, and it was also clear that the group held a range of positions on this, as might be expected from the way the group was set up. Some expressed the conviction that the texts were referring to certain categories of same-sex behaviour, including abusive (gang rape, prostitution and pederasty), perverse (deviating from natural inclination) and cultic (temple ritual) forms, and that the morality of a loving, committed same-sex partnership is not in view at all. Some held that at least some of the references seem to speak to same-sex behaviour across the board – such as the reference in Romans 1 to that which is 'natural' and 'unnatural'[52] – and felt that the traditional interpretations of these passages were to be held with due respect until evidence to the contrary was compelling. Others felt unsure – challenged by the revisionist views, but not wholly convinced.

FOCUS: On the Condemning Texts

There are seven passages in the Bible that refer directly to same-sex erotic behaviours.

Genesis 19:1–13 (see also Judges 19:1–30)

The two angels arrived at Sodom in the evening, and Lot was sitting in the gateway of the city. When he saw them, he got up to meet them and bowed down with his face to the ground. 'My lords,' he said, 'please turn aside to your servant's house. You can wash your feet and spend the night and then go on your way early in the morning.' 'No,' they answered, 'we will spend the night in the square.' But he insisted so strongly that they did go with him and entered his house. He prepared a meal for them, baking bread without yeast, and they ate.

Before they had gone to bed, all the men from every part of the city of Sodom – both young and old – surrounded the house. They called to Lot, 'Where are the men who came to you tonight? Bring them out to us so that we can have sex with them.' Lot went outside to meet them and shut the door behind him and said, 'No, my friends. Don't do this wicked thing. Look, I have two daughters who have never slept with a man. Let me bring them out to you, and you can do what you like with them. But don't do anything to these men, for they have come under the protection of my roof.' 'Get out of our way,' they replied. 'This fellow came here as a foreigner, and now he wants to play the judge! We'll treat you worse than them.' They kept bringing pressure on Lot and moved forward to break down the door. But the men inside reached out and pulled Lot back into the house and shut the door. Then they struck the men who were at the door of the house, young and old, with blindness so that they could not find the door.

The two men said to Lot, 'Do you have anyone else here – sons-in-law, sons or daughters, or anyone else in the city who belongs to you? Get them out of here, because we are going to destroy this place. The outcry of the Lord against its people is so great that he has sent us to destroy it.'

The story of Sodom and Gomorrah is deeply shocking to read, with the most shocking detail for modern ears being Lot's offer of his daughters to a marauding crowd (all men) who are intent on forcing themselves sexually on his male visitors (Genesis 19: 6–8). There is a story in the book of Judges (19:1–30) that bears many similarities to this one, in which a crowd of men demand that a traveller is brought out to them that they might 'know him' (19:22), and women are offered for sexual gratification to divert them from their intentions (19:23–24).[53]

There are numerous discussions among biblical commentators concerning what is to be understood from Lot's appeal to the men who are banging at his door, 'Don't do this wicked thing' (v. 7). For while it may seem obvious to the modern reader (the threat of sexual violence), it is often pointed out that the offensiveness of the threatened action may lie in a breach of hospitality, for it was a near sacred duty within Lot's cultural setting to protect and care for those who came under one's roof.[54] This does not take away, of course, the violent and ugly nature of the actions threatened, but it may give pause to locating the strength of Lot's appeal in a revulsion to the homosexual act per se – rather, it is likely to be the violent abuse of guests that is the 'wicked thing'. While the homosexual act is popularly associated with Sodom and Gomorrah (the word 'sodomy' being derived from Sodom), other Old Testament references point to the sins of injustice, pride, greed and a neglect of the poor[55] – a combination that Walter Brueggemann sums up as a 'general disorder of a society organised against God'.[56]

What are we to make of these harrowing tales, and what bearing might they have on the contemporary issue of same-sex relationships? Referring to the story of Sodom and Gomorrah, Richard Hays states boldly that it is simply 'irrelevant to the topic (of same-sex consensual relationships)'.[57] Many other traditionalists would agree – the threat of gang rape, aimed at men and carried out (in one case) on a woman, surely has no bearing on how we regard those who live in loving, committed, same-sex relationships. Our discussion on this passage might easily end there. However, Brownson, while agreeing with Hays, suggests that the two stories might throw some light on the antipathy shown elsewhere in the Bible to sexual relations between men.[58] Brownson is keen to point out the 'limited moral vision' inherent in the stories, in which the rape of a woman is considered less heinous than the rape of a man. He argues that this expresses a strong patriarchal outlook in which women hold a much lower status to men, which, in turn, helps to explain why a same-sex act would have been so offensive to ancients – since it put the passive partner into the role or place of a woman, thus reducing him to a lower status. These are themes worth keeping in mind as we move to the other 'condemning passages'.

LEVITICUS 18:22 & 20:13

Do not have sexual relations with a man as one does with a woman; that is detestable… If a man has sexual relations with a man as one does with a woman, both of them have done what is detestable. They are to be put to death; their blood will be on their own heads.

These verses are part of the holiness code that is part of the Covenant of Yahweh with Israel. The code expresses in detail what it means for Israel to be set apart to God and distinctive in the world. As Gordon Fee has reminded us, this is not our (Gentile believers) covenant and we are under no obligation to obey its stipulations except where they are renewed in the New Covenant.[59] Yet, we understand that the code has value for us in revealing God's character and what it means for us to live as his people, so long as we recognise its cultural setting and seek to discern between enduring principles and their cultural expressions. Most see in the law code a mix of ethical and ritual laws, and it is easy to spot the stipulations we have deemed unnecessary to fulfil in our day – including regulations about cutting hair (19:27), wearing mixed fabrics (19:19), and what to plant in one's field (19:19). Many of the stipulations do have a moral sense to them – including those concerning sexual relations. Bestiality, incest and adultery are all prohibited, along with 'having sexual relations with a man as one does with a woman' (18:22 and 20:13), which is declared to be 'detestable', warranting the death penalty for both men involved.

Hays states that this prohibition is unambiguous and 'stands as the foundation for the subsequent universal rejection of male same-sex intercourse within Judaism.'[60] Yet he adds that its relevance for Christian ethics can only be decided by looking at how the New Testament writers treated it – that is, did they affirm it or leave it behind?

Others have not been content to simply feel the clarity and force of the prohibition against male same-sex behaviour, and have sought to penetrate the moral logic behind it. There are three aspects frequently explored. Firstly, it is observed that one rationale of the law code was to keep God's people from imitating the practices of those around them (see 20:23–24). Brownson points out that the word translated 'detestable' or 'abomination' is closely linked to idolatrous practices in at least thirty-nine other passages in Scripture.[61] On the strength of this, the IVP New Bible Dictionary takes the view that the prohibitions against male-to-male sex in Leviticus, understood in context, are aimed primarily at idolatrous practices, and are not necessarily to be given wider application.[62] Secondly, concerns with procreation are detected in the text, leading to the idea that homosexual behaviour might be seen negatively because it cannot lead to childbirth. Thirdly, there is Brownson's contention that the prohibitions are essentially about male honour in a patriarchal society, where a male taking a female role and being penetrated by another male would have been considered disgraceful, due to the status of the male being acted upon being lowered to that of a woman. If Brownson is right, this might also explain why there is no female-to-female equivalent prohibition, as there is for bestiality (20:15–16), since 'there is no such degradation operative in these cases'.[63]

The upshot of these points, either separately or in combination, is the assertion that the prohibitions in the text have a limited reference, either to the sexual conduct around pagan temple worship and/or to the particular values and sensibilities of the patriarchal society to which they were addressed. Thus, it might be argued that we cannot read them as timeless ordinances. Many would disagree with this assertion, countering that the moral logic underlying them is not exhausted by cultic associations or particular cultural forms, and would agree with Hays that we need to turn to the New Testament to see what decisions are made there about the relevance of these moral commands to Christian ethics.

1 CORINTHIANS 6:9–10

Or do you not know that wrongdoers will not inherit the kingdom of God? Do not be deceived: neither the sexually immoral nor idolaters nor adulterers nor male prostitutes nor practising homosexuals nor thieves nor the greedy nor drunkards nor slanderers nor swindlers will inherit the kingdom of God.

In 1 Corinthians, Paul writes to a community that it seems had begun to think their spiritual life in Christ made it unimportant what they did with their bodies (6:18–20). 'Do not be deceived,' says Paul, 'neither the sexually immoral nor idolaters nor adulterers nor male prostitutes nor practising homosexuals…will inherit the kingdom God' (6:9,10). Now the Greek words translated 'male prostitutes' and 'practising homosexuals' in the TNIV are *malakoi* (denoting 'soft' or 'feminine') and *arsenokoitai* (literally 'sleepers with men' or 'men-bedders'). It is important to realise that neither of these are technical terms meaning 'homosexuals', since no such word exists in Hebrew, nor was there such a concept of human identity in the ancient world. *Malakoi* was used in Hellenistic Greek as pejorative slang to describe the 'passive' partners – often young boys – in same-sex erotic activity. *Arsenokoitai* is not found in any extra-biblical sources earlier than 1 Corinthians, yet its literal meaning and its proximity to *malakoi* in the list has suggested to some that it refers to the active partner in pederasty. Reflecting on the placement of the two words in Paul's list, Jerome Murphy O' Connor writes:

> At first sight these do not seem to fit with the other vices because sometimes homosexual relationships are models of enduring affection. In reality, however, the terms suggest an effeminate call-boy who is used by an older sodomite. This was the most common form of homosexuality in the ancient world, and was viciously exploited on both sides. Thus for Paul it typified the degenerate relationships that characterised society. [64]

In his discussion of *arsenokoitai*, Hays cites the work of Robin Scroggs who has shown that the word is a translation of the Hebrew *mishkav zakur* ('lying with a male') derived directly from Leviticus 18:22 and 20:13. [65] Hays underlines the importance of this connection, asserting that it demonstrates an affirmation by the apostle Paul of the longstanding negative assessment of male same-sex erotic behaviour, which thereby continues to be valid in the New Testament era.[66]

Hays' point is convincingly made, yet this hardly establishes *arsenokoitai* as a blanket term for any form of homosexual behaviour. In the context, it most likely points to well-known and common practices in the day, including male prostitution, sexual rituals in the pagan temples, and pederasty – the latter being widespread in the ancient Grecian and Roman world, and a pastoral issue within churches whose membership included slaves, many of whom would have been the passive partners in such arrangements.[67]

1 TIMOTHY 1:9–10A

We also know that the law is made not for the righteous but for lawbreakers and rebels, the ungodly and sinful, the unholy and irreligious, for those who kill their fathers or mothers, for murderers, for the sexually immoral, for those practising homosexuality, for slave traders and liars and perjurers.

In 1 Timothy 1:10 we find another vice-list including *arsenokoitai*. While *malakoi* is not present, two other words *pornoi* ('fornicators' or possibly 'male prostitutes') and *andropodistai* ('slave dealers' or 'kidnappers'), might, in combination, refer to a particularly sordid arrangement: namely 'slave dealers acting as pimps for their captured and castrated boys servicing the *arsenokoitai*, the men who made use of them.'[68] Such practices have a modern equivalent in people trafficking, which is surely just as deserving of inclusion in Paul's vice-list, alongside those who murder their parents, murderers, liars and perjurers. Whereas, it seems incongruent to place loving, same-sex partnerships in the same list, which is effectively what we do if *arsenokoitai* is made a reference to all forms of homosexual behaviour. This would seem to be a category error. We cannot of course know for certain what was in the mind of Paul when he wrote what he did. It is likely, as Timothy Keller argues, that 'as a cultured and travelled Roman Citizen, Paul would have been very familiar with long-term, stable, loving relationships between same-sex couples.'[69] Yet the language and tone used by Paul does not seem to point us in this direction, but rather to the kind of relationships where one man dominated another sexually and others made a profit from it.

ROMANS 1:18–32

The wrath of God is being revealed from heaven against all the godlessness and wickedness of human beings who suppress the truth by their wickedness, since what may be known about God is plain to them, because God has made it plain to them. For since the creation of the world God's invisible qualities – his eternal power and divine nature – have been clearly seen, being understood from what has been made, so that people are without excuse.

For although they knew God, they neither glorified him as God nor gave thanks to him, but their thinking became futile and their foolish hearts were darkened. Although they claimed to be wise, they became fools and exchanged the glory of the immortal God for images made to look like mortal human beings and birds and animals and reptiles.

Therefore God gave them over in the sinful desires of their hearts to sexual impurity for the degrading of their bodies with one another. They exchanged the truth about God for a lie, and worshipped and served created things rather than the Creator – who is for ever praised, Amen.

Because of this, God gave them over to shameful lusts. Even their women exchanged natural sexual relations for unnatural ones. In the same way the men also abandoned natural relations with women and were inflamed with lust for one another. Men committed shameful acts with other men, and received in themselves the due penalty for their error.

Furthermore, just as they did not think it worthwhile to retain the knowledge of God, so God gave them over to a depraved mind, so that they do what ought not to be done. They have become filled with every kind of wickedness, evil, greed and depravity. They are full of envy, murder, strife, deceit and malice. They are gossips, slanderers, God-haters, insolent, arrogant and boastful; they invent ways of doing evil; they disobey their parents; they have no understanding, no fidelity, no love, no mercy. Although they know God's righteous decree that those who do such things deserve death, they not only continue to do these very things but also approve of those who practise them.

At an early stage in his articulation of the gospel in the book of Romans, Paul launches into a polemic against the wickedness of the pagan (non-Jewish) world that would have been quite familiar to his Jewish readers: just the kind of rhetoric that other Jewish writers and Stoic Philosophers engaged in at the time. The essential approach of all such denouncements was to trace all the sinful and destructive features of society to idolatry: to worshipping created things rather than the Creator. In Paul's handling, the consequences of this fundamental sin are played out progressively in those who, having exchanged the truth of God for a lie, give themselves to shameful and degrading sexual acts.

Because of this, God gave them over to shameful lusts. Even their women exchanged natural relations for unnatural ones. In the same way the men also abandoned natural relations with women and were inflamed with lust for one another. Men committed shameful acts with other men, and received in themselves the due penalty for their error.[70]

James Alison has reflected on this process, from idolatry through deception to degradation, and has posited that it is framed entirely within the context of pagan worship.[71] Thus, for Alison, references to 'unnatural' sexual behaviour point to the frenzied sexual antics that went on in and around the pagan temples throughout the Mediterranean world in Paul's day. Alison cites the cults of Cybele, Atys and Aphrodite, whose largest temple was in Corinth where Paul most probably wrote his letter to Rome, and describes rites that involved cross-dressing and orgiastic frenzies in which men allowed themselves to be penetrated, often culminating in some men castrating themselves and becoming eunuchs.

Alison's analysis is worthy of consideration, given that the heart of Paul's diagnosis of sinful humankind is misplaced worship. If he is right, then the reference to same-sex behaviour is quite specific and would have little bearing on loving, same-sex relationships today. However, it seems likely that Paul's intended reference was wider than this – including at least the common practices of male-prostitution and pederasty, as described in the discussion of the 'vice-lists' above, for these can just as easily be seen as outcomes of misplaced worship, and concord with the out of control, lust-driven sexual behaviour portrayed in the passage. The question – as with the other texts discussed above – is whether we can legitimately extend these denouncements to loving, same-sex relationships.

Richard Hays is among those who see deeper and wider implications in the text. He argues that Paul's depiction of the pagan world turning from worshipping the Creator to images of created things would certainly have evoked the creation narrative for his Jewish readers. Hays argues that they would have seen the abandonment of God-ordained gender roles through unnatural sexual behaviour as a clear sign of rebellion – 'a sacrament (so to speak) of the anti-religion of human beings who refuse to honour God as Creator […] an outward and visible sign of an inward and spiritual reality – the rejection of the Creator's design.' [72]

A main point of contention between traditionalists and revisionists in Romans 1 is the meaning of the Greek word *physis* ('nature'). Traditionalists understand the term, in Paul's use and in extra-biblical literature, to mean the natural order of creation – that is, what God has designed and purposed in creation – including the biological complementarity of male and female. (In Hellenistic Judaism, the God-given order, manifest in Creation, was considered to be perfectly aligned with the Law of Moses.)

Some revisionists have offered the alternative interpretation of *physis* as what is *natural to each individual,* implying that what Paul is addressing in Romans 1:26–27 is perversion (people moving against their natural orientation) and so cannot be applied to those whose orientation is homosexual. Hays objects that this is to 'lapse into anachronism', since the notion of 'orientation' was not in the ancient mindset.[73] He is surely right in this. However, Brownson argues that while they may have had little concept of sexual orientation, the ancients did have a sense of what was natural to the individual, which was for a man to desire a woman and to unite with her in marriage for procreation. Brownson argues that this was one strand in a three-stranded understanding of what was 'natural' (or according to nature). Firstly, there was personal disposition (with no conception of same-sex orientation); secondly there was the created order; and thirdly there was social convention. The last of these might be illustrated by Paul's contention elsewhere that it is 'against nature' for a man to wear his hair long, which cannot be read easily as an appeal to the created order (1 Corinthians 11:14). Brownson refers to this text, and goes on to argue that social convention is also implicit in Paul's reference to what is natural in Romans: including a patriarchal outlook that placed women below men and would have viewed a male to male sexual act as the degrading of the passive partner, since it lowered his status to that of a woman (as discussed above). For Brownson, the convergence of personal, communal and cosmic aspects in determining what is 'natural' enables people to work out what it means to live well (that is, in God's way) in the world – and this convergence, he argues, will not be the same for us in the twentieth century as it was for the first century church. Thus, our less patriarchal more egalitarian culture, and our understanding of sexuality, as informed by the scientific studies referenced earlier, will lead us to a different sense of what it means to live according 'nature'; that is, to live in God's way.

Brownson has put up some good arguments for a revised reading of Romans 1, backed by thorough investigation of the biblical text, and has given a credible challenge to the traditionalist view on same-sex unions. This by no means decides the matter, and our discussion only really scratches the surface of the debate. Yet enough has been indicated in relation to Romans 1 and to the other texts considered, to venture that both traditionalist and revisionist readings are tenable within a conversation premised on a high view of Scripture. In particular, I believe it is reasonable to take the view that the texts refer to particular forms of same-sex erotic behaviour and have no bearing on the loving, same-sex unions about which we are concerned; just as it is reasonable to see a wider reference and application. In the end, the matter will not be decided within the limited territory of a handful of verses. We need to look beyond them to the whole witness of Scripture.

SEXUALITY, FAITH & THE ART OF CONVERSATION

PARTS TWO, THREE & FOUR – INTRODUCTION

A Few Words To Begin

Sometimes Christians disagree – in doctrine, ethics, and matters more pragmatic. If you doubt me, take a look at any century of church history, or spend a year in any Christian community.

How do we understand this, as the community to whom Christ gave the Spirit to lead us into all truth?

We might suppose that some followers of Jesus are not reading their Bibles, or have simply failed to understand the meaning or implications of the Scriptures correctly, perhaps out of spiritual immaturity. Yet what if both sides on some disagreement study the Scriptures with due diligence, looking to the Spirit to guide them, and still arrive at different conclusions? What then?

Perhaps you or I might write an article, or even a book, to state and defend our view. Or we might leave the church community that does not see things as we do (assuming I agree with you!) to find one that does – creating a little distance to keep the faith. Or maybe start a new movement or denomination, if the issue seems important enough. Alternatively, we might try a conversation.

In February 2013, a dozen people at Bookham Baptist Church began a conversation. It was all about how a local church might respond to those who are same-sex attracted and seeking to follow

Jesus. We were a mixed bunch: recruited to include a good range of viewpoints on what constitutes a biblical understanding of same-sex attraction and relationships. We had about six months, after which we were to bring the fruit of our endeavours to a meeting of the members of our church.

'Sexuality, Faith & the Art of Conversation: Part One' (hereafter, *SFAC1*), related the early stages of our conversation, interweaving focus pieces (short essays), interviews and fictional conversations set in the Wild Goose Coffee Shop. This follow up volume (Parts 2–4) continues to relate the conversation of the group up to and beyond the church meeting that received our report, and follows how the conversation widened and deepened within our church community.

Wherever you are in your journey of faith, and whatever your sexuality or gender, I would like to welcome you to this conversation. *Come and join in.* There is room for you. Along the way I have included some prompts to pause and reflect (headed 'Join the Conversation'), and I hope you will. There are even a few blank pages that might prove useful for jotting down your thoughts (created because I have a thing about starting each new chapter on the right hand side – an author's quirk!). If you have not read my first book (*SFAC1*), it might be as well to start there – although now that I have your attention, it is very tempting to encourage you to read on and get your bearings as you go. Often it is like that when we join a conversation. I will leave it up to you.

No doubt some of you would like to know how it all ends before starting on the journey. You can always flip to the end, of course; though I wouldn't recommend it. The fruits of our endeavours are not all located there, but in several places along the way. My advice would be to commit to the journey and see where it takes you.

Join the conversation…

*How good and pleasant it is when God's
people live together in unity!*
(Psalm 133:1)

NOTES

1 Celtic Daily Prayer, From the Northumbrian Community (London, Harper Collins, 2000), p. 20.

INTRODUCTION

2 https://www.bathandwells.org.uk/event/revd-nick-bundock-beyond-inclusion-lizzie-lowes-story/
3 In the main, my research has concerned same-sex attraction, which is the focus of this booklet. However, implications for other groups within the LGBT+ population begin to be explored in my second book (available Easter 2019).
4 Stephen Elmes, *Sexuality, Faith & the Art of Conversation – Part One* (Surrey, Creative Tension Publications, 2017). Parts Two, Three & Four (in one volume) are now available.
5 While some aspects of the story told within these pages reflect the Baptist tradition, its main ideas are, I believe, accessible and translatable to other traditions. I have aimed towards a broad readership, including those who are not part of a church community.

SCENE ONE

6 Leviticus 18:22 and 20:13.
7 Genesis 19:1-13.
8 1 Corinthians 6:9-10, 1 Timothy 1:9-10a, Romans 1:18-32.
9 Most evangelical scholars today support this view, though not all (see resources on pp. 27-28).
10 Genesis 2:24, Mark 10:8.

SCENE TWO

11 Genesis 2:24, Mark 10:8.
12 Mary and Nigel's comments signal the importance of listening to and learning from the experiences of those who are same-sex attracted. If we fail in this, our conversation could easily become an academic exercise.

SCENE THREE

13 Isaiah 56:3-8.
14 Acts 11:1-18.
15 Genesis 12:1-3.

SCENE FOUR

16 The story of Shaz and Davina is not meant to represent a particular couple or their church situation, but is based on a number of people and situations I have been involved with. It is given to stimulate discussion.
17 Acts 2:37-41, Acts 8:9-13, Acts 9:17-19, Acts 10:44-46, Acts 19:1-7.

SCENE FIVE

18 This phrase is taken from a longstanding, Baptist Covenant prayer, included in the Baptist Union's *Gathering for Worship: Patterns and Prayers for the Community of Disciples* (Ed. Christopher Ellis and Myra Blyth, Norwich, Canterbury Press, 2005), p. 37.

19 I have had go at thinking this through in my second book, *Sexuality, Faith & the Art of Conversation – Parts Two, Three & Four* (Surrey UK, Creative Tension Publications, 2019), pp. 289–292.

RESOURCES FOR DELVING DEEPER

20 Robert A. Gagnon, *The Bible and Homosexual Practice: Texts and Hermeneutics* (Nashville, 2001, Abingdon Press).
21 Matthew Vines, *God and the Gay Christian: The Biblical Case in Support of Same-Sex Relationships* (New York, 2014, Crown Publishing).
22 James V. Brownson, *Bible Gender Sexuality: Reframing the Church's Debate on Same-Sex Relationships* (Grand Rapids, MI, Eerdmanns Publishing, 2013).
23 Preston Sprinkle, *Two views on Homosexuality, the Bible and the Church,* (Zondervan, 2016).
24 Andrew Marin, *Love Is an Orientation: Elevating the Conversation with the Gay Community* (Downers Grove, IL, InterVarsity Press, 2009).
25 Wesley Hill, *Washed and Waiting: Reflections on Christian Faithfulness and Homosexuality* (Grand Rapids: Zondervan, 2010).

26 Vicky Beeching, *Undivided: Coming Out, Becoming Whole, and Living Free of Shame* (London, Harper Collins, 2018).

27 Mark Greene, Executive Director of the London Institute for Contemporary Christianity (LICC).

SEXUALITY, FAITH & THE ART OF CONVERSATION – PART ONE

CHAPTER 4

28 Baptist Union Human Sexuality Working Group, *Baptists Exploring Issues of Homosexuality: How Baptists Might Think Biblically and Theologically about Homosexuality.* Papers for the Educational Process, extended and formatted for use by Stephen Elmes for the facilitation of conversations in churches.

29 Baptist Union, *Declaration of Principle*
http://www.baptist.org.uk/Groups/220595/Declaration_of_Principle.aspx.

30 See Chapter 7 – Framing the Same Sex Discussion…

31 For a good overview see Carl S. Keener and Douglas E. Swartzendruber, 'The Biological Basis of Homosexuality' in *To Continue the Dialogue: Biblical Interpretation and Homosexuality*, ed. by C. Normal Krause, Living Issues Series, I (Ontario: Pandora Press, 2001), 148–173 (pp.151–164).

32 Stanton L. Jones and Mark A. Yarhouse, *Homosexuality: The Use of Scientific Research in the Church's Moral Debate* (Illinois, InterVarsity Press, 2000), pp. 47–91.

33 Please note that this section (pp. 50–52) has recently been edited (February 2020) to include the insights of the Geneticist, Francis Collins and to add a reflection about the ethics and wisdom of supporting a person towards a change of sexual orientation.

34 Carl Keener and Douglas E. Swartzentruber, p. 150.

35 Jones and Yarhouse, pp. 81–83.

36 Jones and Yarhouse, pp. 83–84.

37 Francis Collins, *The Language of God: A Scientist Presents Evidence for Belief* (London, Simon & Schuster UK, 2006), p. 260.

38 Lawrence S. Mayer and Paul R. McHugh, Sexuality and Gender: Findings from the Biological, Psychological, and Social Services in *The New Atlantis: A Journal of Technology and Society* (No. 50 – Fall 2016), p. 7.

39 Mayer and McHugh, p. 7.

40 A point made by Collins in correspondence with Warren Throckmorton, Professor of Psychology at Grove City College:
https://www.wthrockmorton.com/2008/09/30/what-did-francis-collins-really-say-about-homosexuality [accessed 31/01/20].

41 Leanne Payne, *The Broken Image: Restoring Sexual Wholeness Through Healing Prayer*, 1st British edition (Eastbourne: Kingsway Publications Ltd, 1989.

42 Jeremy Marks, *Exchanging the Truth of God for a Lie: One man's spiritual journey to find the truth about homosexuality and same–sex partnerships*, second edn (Surrey: Courage UK, 2009), p. 6.

43 Marks, pp. 55–58.

44 Medical journals have long ceased referring to homosexuality as an illness or disorder, and therapies that aim to effect a change of sexual orientation are generally deemed unethical. See Joseph Nicolosi, *Reparative Therapy of Male Homosexuality: A New Clinical Approach* (Oxford, Rowman & Littlefield Publishers Inc., 1991), pp. 7–24 for some helpful reflections on the history and politics of diagnosis in relation to sexuality.

45 Jones and Yarhouse, p. 133.

46 Jones and Yarhouse, p. 148.

47 See for example: https://bmcpsychiatry.biomedcentral.com/articles/10.1186/1471-244X-9-11 [accessed 13/02/20] and https://pcc-cic.org.uk/article/nhs-england-clarifies-its-stance-conversion-therapy [accessed 13/02/20].

48 Baptist Union Human Sexuality Working Group, Section entitled 'Sexual Diversity', Table: *Reported homosexual and heterosexual attraction and experience.* More recent and extensive data can be obtained from The Lancet (free registration required), *Sexual Behaviour in Britain: Partnerships, Practices and HIV risk behaviours*, by Anne M. Johnson and others, Table 4, http://www.thelancet.com/journals/lancet/article/PIIS0140–6736(01)06883–0/fulltext#back–bib1 and on the Natsal (National Survey of Sexual Attitudes and Lifestyle) website, which provides comparison of surveys in 1990 (Natsal–1), 2000 (Natsal–2) and 2010 (Natsal–3), http://www.natsal.ac.uk/home.aspx.

49 Mona Chalabi, *Gay Britain: what do the statistics say?* (The Guardian, Thursday 3 October, 2013) http://www.theguardian.com/politics/reality–check/2013/oct/03/gay–britain–what–do–statistics–say.

50 Rose Eveleth, *What Percentage of the Population is Gay? More Than You Think* (Smithsonian.com, October 2013) http://www.smithsonianmag.com/smart–news/what–percent–of–the–population–is–gay–more–than–you–think–5012467/?no–ist

51 The Lancet.com http://www.thelancet.com/action/showFullTableImage?tableId=tbl4&pii=S0140673613620358.

CHAPTER 5

52 Romans 1:26–27.

53 I am counting the story in Judges 19 as one of the seven passages.

54 Jesus' reference to Sodom and Gomorrah in Matthew 10:15 certainly places what happened in the context of hospitality, though in the letter to Jude (v. 7), the emphasis is clearly on sexual immorality.

55 Isaiah 1:10; 3:9; Jeremiah 23:14, Ezekiel 16:49.

56 Walter Brueggemann, *Genesis*, Interpretation: A Bible Series for Teaching and Preaching (Atlanta, John Knox Press, 1982), p. 164.

57 Richard B. Hays, *The Moral Vision of the New Testament: Community, Cross, New Creation: A Contemporary Introduction to New Testament* (New York, NY, HarperCollins, 1996), p. 381.

58 James V. Brownson, *Bible Gender Sexuality: Reframing the Church's Debate on Same–Sex Relationships* (Grand Rapids, MI, Eerdmanns Publishing, 2013) p. 268.

59 Gordon D. Fee & Douglas Stuart, *How to Read the Bible for All its Worth*, 2nd edition (Grand Rapids, MI, Scripture Union, 1994) pp. 151–2.

60 Hays, p. 381.

61 Brownson, p. 270.

62 *IVP New Bible Dictionary*, ed. By J. D. Douglas and others, 2nd edition (Leicester, Inter–Varsity Press, 1982) p. 488.

63 Brownson, p. 272.

64 Jerome Murphy O'Connor, *1 Corinthians*, The People's Bible Commentary (Oxford, The Bible Reading Fellowship, 1997) p. 59.

65 Q. in Hays, 382.

66 Hays, p. 383.

67 The original sentence in *Sexuality, Faith & the Art of Conversation: Part One* suggested pederasty as the most likely reference of *arsenokoitai*. Here I have indicated other possibilities too (edited February 2020).

68 Brownson, p. 274.

69 Timothy Keller, *Romans 1–7 For You* (New Malden, UK: The Good Book Company, 2014) p. 32.

70 Romans 1:26–27.

71 James Alison, 'But the Bible says…' A Catholic Reading of Romans 1 (2004), http://www.jamesalison.co.uk/texts/eng15.html.

72 Hays, p. 26–27.

73 Hays, p. 389.

Printed in Great Britain
by Amazon

44768118R00051